YOU GIVE LOVE A BAD NAME

YOU GIVE LOVE A BAD NAME

Timeless Poems of Tainted Love

from the Pop Hits of the '70s and '80s

Edited by Danny Cassidy

QUIRK BOOKS

PHILADELPHIA

Library of Congress Cataloging in Publication Number: 2003090707

ISBN 1-931686-13-0

Printed in Singapore

Typeset in New Garden and GillSans

Designed by Karen Onorato
Cover Photography by Andrea Stephany

Photographs on pages 21, 52, and 75 courtesy of Index Stock Imagery
Photographs on pages 34 and 65 courtesy of Getty Images

Additional copyright information begins on page 92

Distributed in North America by Chronicle Books
85 Second Street
San Francisco, CA 94105

10 9 8 7 6 5 4 3 2 1

Quirk Books
215 Church Street
Philadelphia, PA 19106
www.quirkbooks.com

Contents

Introduction

Breaking up is hard to do—and when disaster strikes, we all seek comfort in different ways. Some indulge in pints of Häagen-Dazs. Others indulge in pints of Guinness. Still others rush out and buy nauseating self-help books with titles like *How to Win Him Back in Forty-Eight Hours or Less.*

But not me. When I have a broken heart, I just turn up the radio, because pop music gives me all the consolation I need. The lyrics collected in this anthology have helped me overcome many a difficult breakup. They remind me that I'm not alone—even Bon Jovi and Whitney Houston have felt the painful sting of rejection.

Major breakups are traumatic experiences. Psychiatrist Elisabeth Kübler Ross believed that we pass through five stages after receiving catastrophic news. The first of these stages is *denial.* When we learn that a loved one is abandoning us, we are often too blindsided to accept the information as fact. Joe Jackson grapples with this kind of shock when he asks, "Is she really going out with him? / Is she really going to take him home tonight?" He is so confused, he even raises the possibility that he might be hallucinating: "'Cause if my eyes don't deceive me / there's something going wrong around here."

From denial, most people quickly transition to the next stage: *anger*. The ex-boyfriend or ex-girlfriend is frequently a target of this rage. Bon Jovi compares his anguish to homicide: "Shot through the heart / and you're to blame, darling. / You give love a bad name." The more introspective Joan Jett, on the other hand, directs her rage inward. "I hate myself for loving you," she writes. "Can't break free of the things that you do."

No matter how angry these lovers seem, most harbor hopes that the relationship will endure. The third stage, *bargaining*, concerns their desperate attempts at reconciliation. "If ever you're in my arms again," Peabo Bryson promises, "this time I'll love you much better." Player accepts full responsibility for the breakup and pleads for a second chance: "Baby come back," he writes. "You can blame it all on me. / I was wrong, and I just can't live without you."

When these attempts fail, a person will sink into the fourth and longest stage: *depression*. "Every now and then I get a little bit tired of listening to the sound of my tears," Bonnie Tyler writes, and Barry Manilow finds that his world no longer makes sense: "Caught up in a world / of uphill climbing. / The tears are in my eyes, / And nothing is rhyming." The fact that "climbing" and "rhyming" *do* rhyme suggests that Manilow has lost any sense of self-awareness. Hall and Oates echo a similar despair when they write, "Think I'll spend eternity in the city. / Let the carbon and monoxide choke my thoughts away, yeah."

While painful and frequently unbearable, these first four stages are necessary to arrive at the fifth—and most triumphant—stage, that of *acceptance*. When Lisa Lisa explains she is "all cried out" over her lover, we know she is ready to move on. Even Patty Smyth of Scandal learns to view her breakup as a positive change: "These last few weeks of holding on— / the days are dull, the nights are long / Guess it's better to say: / Goodbye to you."

So if you find yourself coping with a broken heart, let the poetry in this anthology be your moral compass. Yes, love *is* a battlefield. Love stinks, love bites, love is just a second-hand emotion. But you're not alone. All of these pop stars have suffered broken hearts, and they've mapped the territory for you. Follow their words through the five stages as quickly as you can—and then say goodbye to all the maneaters and cold-hearted snakes in your life.

It's time to move on.

Is She Really Going Out with Him?

Joe Jackson

Pretty women out walking with gorillas down my street.
From my window I'm staring while my coffee grows cold.
Look over there.
>   Where?
There, there's a lady that I used to know.
She's married now or engaged or something so I'm told.

Is she really going out with him?
>   Is she really going to take him home tonight?
Is she really going out with him?
>   'Cause if my eyes don't deceive me,
>   there's something going wrong around here.

Tonight's the night when I go to all the parties down my street.
I wash my hair and I kid myself I look real smooth.
Look over there.
>   Where?
There, here comes Jeannie with her new boyfriend.
They say that looks don't count for much and so there goes
>   your proof.

Is she really going out with him?
>   Is she really going to take him home tonight?

Is she really going out with him?
>   'Cause if my eyes don't deceive me
>   there's something going wrong around here.
>   Around here.

But if looks could kill,
>   there's a man there who's
>   >   marked down as dead.
>   'Cause I've had my fill.
Listen you,
>   take your hands from her hand.
I get so mean around this scene.
>   Hey, yeah, hey.

Is she really going out with him?

>   Is she really going to take him home tonight?
Is she really going out with him?
>   'Cause if my eyes don't deceive me
>   there's something going wrong around here.
>   Around here.

Something gone wrong around here.
Something gone wrong around here.
Something gone wrong around here.
Something gone wrong around.

Missing You

John Waite

Every time I think of you,
    I always catch my breath.
And I'm still standing here and you're miles away,
    and I'm wondering why you left.
And there's a storm that's raging
    through my frozen heart tonight.

I hear your name in certain circles
    and it always makes me smile.
I spend my time thinking about you,
    and it's almost driving me wild.
And there's a heart that's breaking
    down this long-distance line tonight.

I ain't missing you at all
    since you've been gone away.
I ain't missing you
    no matter what I might say.

There's a message in the wild,
    and I'm sending you this signal tonight.
You don't know how desperate I've become,
    and it looks like I'm losing this fight.

In your world, I have no meaning,
        though I'm trying hard to understand.
And it's my heart that's breaking
        down this long-distance line tonight.

I ain't missing you at all
        since you've been gone away.
I ain't missing you
        no matter what my friends say.

And there's a message that I'm sending out
        like a telegraph to your soul.
And if I can't bridge this distance
        stop this heartbreak overload!

I ain't missing you at all
        since you've been gone away.
I ain't missing you
        no matter what my friends say.

I ain't missing you.
I ain't missing you . . .

I Hate Myself for Loving You
Joan Jett and the Blackhearts

Midnight, getting uptight.
    Where are you?
You said you'd meet me.
    Now it's quarter to two.

I know I'm hanging,
but I'm still wanting you.
    Hey, Jack,
it's a fact: They're talking in town.
    I turn my back and you're messing around.
I'm not really jealous—don't like looking like a clown.

I think of you every night and day.
You took my heart,
then you took my pride
    away.

I hate myself for loving you.
    Can't break free from the things that you do.
I want to walk but I run back to you. That's why
    I hate myself for loving you.

Daylight, spent the night
    without you.
But I've been dreaming
    about the loving you do.

I won't be as angry
about the hell you put me through.
    Hey, man,
Bet you can treat me right.
    You just don't know what you was missing last night.
I want to see your face and say, "forget it," just for spite.

I think of you every night and day.
You took my heart,
then you took my pride
    away.

I hate myself for loving you.
    Can't break free from the things that you do.
I want to walk but I run back to you. That's why
    I hate myself for loving you.

I think of you every night and day.
You took my heart,
then you took my pride
away.

I hate myself for loving you.
Can't break free from the things that you do.
I want to walk but I run back to you. That's why
I hate myself for loving you.

I hate myself
for loving you.
I hate myself
for loving you.
I hate myself
for loving you.
I hate myself
for loving you.

You Give Love a Bad Name

Bon Jovi

Shot through the heart
    and you're to blame, darling.
You give love a bad name.

An angel's smile is what you sell.
    You promise me heaven,
        then put me through hell.
Chains of love got a hold on me.
    When passion's a prison,
        you can't break free.

You're a loaded gun, yeah.
    There's nowhere to run.
No one can save me—
    the damage is done.

Shot through the heart
    and you're to blame.
You give love a bad name.

I play my part
    and you play your game.
You give love a bad name.
      You give love a bad name.

You paint your smile on your lips.
    Blood-red nails
        on your fingertips.
A school boy's dream, you act so shy.
    Your very first kiss
        was your first kiss goodbye.

You're a loaded gun.
    There's nowhere to run.
No one can save me—
    the damage is done.

Shot through the heart
    and you're to blame.
You give love a bad name.

I play my part
    and you play your game.
You give love a bad name.
    You give love a bad name.

Cold Hearted

Paula Abdul

He's a cold-hearted snake.
    Look into his eyes.
        Uh, oh—
            he's been telling lies.

He's a lover boy at play.
    He don't play by rules.
        Uh, oh—
            girl, don't play the fool, now.

You're the one giving up the love
    anytime he needs it.
But you turn your back and then he's off
    and running with the crowd.
You're the one to sacrifice
    anything to please him.
Do you really think he thinks about you
    when he's out?

He's a cold-hearted snake.
    Look into his eyes.
        Uh, oh—
            he's been telling lies.

He's a lover boy at play.

He don't play by rules.

Uh, oh—

girl, don't play the fool, now.

It was only late last night,

he was out there sneaking.

Then he called you up to check

that you were waiting by the phone.

All the world's a candy store.

He's been trick or treating.

When it comes to true love, girl, with him

there's no one home.

20

He's a cold-hearted snake.

Look into his eyes.

Uh, oh—

he's been telling lies.

He's a lover boy at play.

He don't play by rules.

Uh, oh—

girl, don't play the fool, now.

You could find somebody better, girl.
     He could only make you cry.
You deserve somebody better, girl.
     He's cold as ice.

How come he can tell you're always number one
     without a doubt
     when he is always squirming
like a little snake under every rock?
You've been working on the love
     and he's been only playing undercover all the while.
          Take another look into his eyes
          and you will only see a reptile.

Maneater

Hall and Oates

She'll only come out at night,
    the lean and hungry type.
Nothing is new, I've seen her here before.
    Watching and waiting,
she's sitting with you, but her eyes are on the door.

So many have paid to see
    what you think you're getting for free.
The woman is wild, a she-cat tamed by the purr of a Jaguar.
    Money's the matter.
If you're in it for love, you ain't gonna get too far.

Oh, oh, here she comes.
    Watch out, boy, she'll chew you up.
Oh, oh, here she comes.
    She's a maneater.

Oh, oh, here she comes.
    Watch out, boy, she'll chew you up.
Oh, oh, here she comes.
    She's a maneater.

I wouldn't if I were you—

    I know what she can do.

She's deadly, man, and she could really rip your world apart

    Mind over matter.

The beauty is there, but a beast is in the heart.

Oh, oh, here she comes.

    Watch out, boy, she'll chew you up.

Oh, oh, here she comes.

    She's a maneater.

Oh, oh, here she comes.

    Watch out, boy, she'll chew you up.

Oh, oh, here she comes.

    She's a maneater.

Love Stinks

J. Geils Band

You love her
but she loves him,
and he loves somebody else.
You just can't win.

And so it goes,
until the day you die.
This thing they call love—
it's gonna make you cry.

I've had the blues,
the reds, and the pinks.
One thing for sure:

Love stinks.
Love stinks.
Yeah, yeah.
Love stinks.
Love stinks.
Yeah, yeah.
Love stinks.

Two by two
and side by side.
Love's gonna find you.
Yes, it is.
You just can't hide.

You'll hear it call.
Your heart will fall,
then love will fly.
It's gonna soar.

I don't care for any Casanova thing.
All I can say is:

Love stinks.
Love stinks.
Yeah, yeah.
Love stinks.
Love stinks.
Yeah, yeah.
Love stinks.

I've been through diamonds.
I've been through minks.
I've been through it all.
Love stinks.

Love Is a Battlefield

Pat Benatar

We are young.
>Heartache to heartache.
We stand.
>No promises, no demands.

Love is a battlefield.

We are strong.
>No one can tell us we're wrong.
Searching our hearts for so long,
>both of us knowing:

Love is a battlefield.

You're making me go.
Then making me stay.
Why do you hurt me so bad?
It would help me to know:
Do I stand in your way?
Or am I the best thing you've had?

Believe me, believe me, I can't tell you why.
But I'm trapped by your love and I'm chained to your side.

We are young.
  Heartache to heartache.
We stand.
  No promises, no demands.

Love is a battlefield.

We are strong.
  No one can tell us we're wrong.
Searching our hearts for so long,
  both of us knowing:

Love is a battlefield.

When I'm losing control,
will you turn me away?
Or touch me deep inside?
And if all this gets old,
will it still feel the same?
There's no way this will die.

But if we get much closer I could lose control.
And if your heart surrenders you'll need me to hold.

We are young.

    Heartache to heartache.

We stand.

    No promises, no demands.

Love is a battlefield.

We are strong.

    No one can tell us we're wrong.

Searching our hearts for so long,

    both of us knowing:

Love is a battlefield.

Circles

Atlantic Starr

Circles, going round in circles.
Circles, going round in circles.

You're taking too much time
    to make up your mind.

Either you love me
    or you don't.

And all the other girls
    in your crazy mixed-up world,

You said you'd drop them
    But you know you won't.

Sometimes I think about forgetting you.
    But it's so, so hard to make that choice.

'Cause boy, with you,
    I go to seventh heaven
    just by the sound of your voice.

Circles, going round in circles.
Circles, going round in circles.

Out of my head, that's where I'm going.
Trying so hard to deal with you.

It's not so easy trying to bear these changes
that you're putting me through.

In my head, there's a ball of confusion,
and I can't figure out just what to do.

I guess my life will keep on going round and round
until I get away from you.

Circles, going round in circles.
You've got me so confused.

Circles, going round in circles.
Can't get away from you . . .

Out of my head, that's where I'm going.
Trying so hard to deal with you.

It's not so easy trying to bear these changes
that you're putting me through.

In my head, there's a ball of confusion,
      and I can't figure out just what to do.

I guess my life will keep on going round and round
      until I get away from you.

Circles, going round in circles.
      You've got me so confused.

Circles, going round in circles.
      Can't get away from you . . .

Cuts Like a Knife

Bryan Adams

Driving home this evening,
    I could've sworn we had it all worked out.
You had this boy believing
    way beyond the shadow of a doubt.

Then I heard it on the street.
    I heard you might have found somebody new.
Well, who is he, baby? Who is he?
    And tell me what he means to you.

    I took it all for granted,
    but how was I to know
    that you'd be letting go?

Now it cuts like a knife,
    but it feels so right.
It cuts like a knife,
    but it feels so right.

There's times I've been mistaken.
    There's times I thought I'd been misunderstood.
So wait a minute, darling.
    Can't you see we did the best we could?

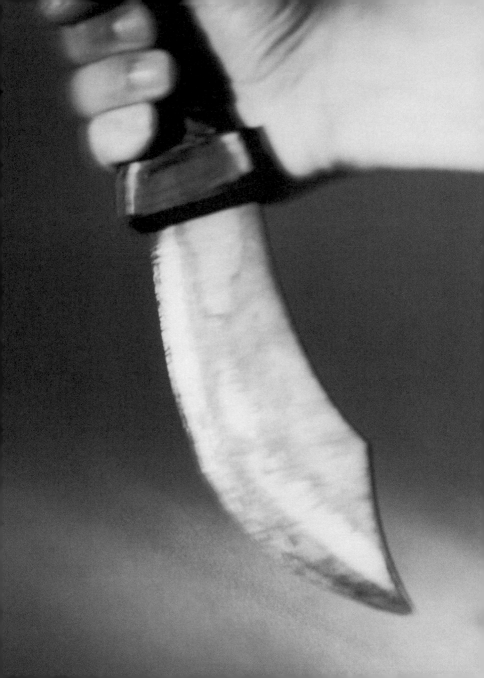

This wouldn't be the first time
      things have gone astray.
      Now you've thrown it all away.

Now it cuts like a knife,
      but it feels so right.
It cuts like a knife,
      but it feels so right.

Don't Do Me Like That

Tom Petty and the Heartbreakers

I was talking with a friend of mine,
    Said a woman had hurt his pride.
Told him that she loved him so
    and turned around and let him go.
Then he said, "You better watch your step,
    or you're gonna get hurt yourself.
Someone's gonna tell you lies,
    cut you down to size."

Don't do me like that.
Don't do me like that.
What if I love you, baby?
Don't do me like that.

Don't do me like that.
Don't do me like that.
Someday I might need you, baby.
Don't do me like that.

Listen, honey, can you see?
    Baby, you would bury me.
If you were in the public eye,
    giving someone else a try.

And you know you better watch your step,
    or you're gonna get hurt yourself.
Someone's gonna tell you lies,
    cut you down to size.

Don't do me like that.
Don't do me like that.
What if I love you, baby?
Don't, don't, don't, don't . . .

'Cause somewhere deep down inside,
    someone is saying, "Love doesn't last that long."
I got this feeling inside night and day
    and now I can't take it no more . . .

If Ever You're in My Arms Again
Peabo Bryson

it all came
so easy,
all the loving you
gave me,
the feelings we shared.

and i still can
remember
how your touch was
so tender,
it told me you cared.

we had a once
in a lifetime
but i just
couldn't see,
until it was
gone.
a second once
in a lifetime
may be too much

to ask but i
swear from
now on:

if ever
you're in my
arms again,
this time
i'll love you
much better.
if ever
you're in my
arms again,
this time
i'll hold you
forever.
this time will
never end.

now i'm seeing
clearly
how i still need you
near me.
i still love you so.

there's something
between us
that won't ever
leave us.
there's no letting go.

we had a once
in a lifetime
but i just
didn't know it
until my life
fell apart.
a second once
in a lifetime
isn't too much
to ask 'cause i
swear from
the heart:

if ever
you're in my
arms again,
this time
i'll love you
much better.

if ever
you're in my
arms again,
this time
i'll hold you
forever.
this time
will never end.
never end.

the best of
romances
deserve second
chances.
i'll get to you
somehow
'cause i promise
now:

if ever
you're in my
arms again,
this time
i'll love you
much better.

if ever
you're in my
arms again,
this time
i'll hold you
forever.
this time
will never end.

Don't Cry Out Loud

Melissa Manchester

Baby cried the day the circus came to town
>'cause she didn't want parades just passing by her.

So she painted on a smile and took up with some clown
>while she danced without a net upon the wire.

I know a lot about her
'cause you see,
Baby is an awful lot like me.

Don't cry out loud.
>Just keep it inside
>and learn how to hide your feelings.

Fly high and proud.
>And if you should fall,
>remember you almost had it all.

Baby saw that when they took the big top down,
>they left behind her dreams among the litter.

And the different kind of love she thought she'd found—
>there was nothing left but sawdust and some glitter.

But Baby can't be broken
'cause you see,
she had the finest teacher—
that was me. I told her:

Don't cry out loud.
　　Just keep it inside
　　and learn how to hide your feelings.
Fly high and proud.
　　And if you should fall,
　　remember you almost had it all.

Don't cry out loud.
　　Just keep it inside
　　and learn how to hide your feelings.
Fly high and proud.
　　And if you should fall,
　　remember you almost made it.

Don't cry out loud.
　　Just keep it inside
　　and learn how to hide your feelings.
Fly high and proud.
　　And if you should fall,
　　remember you almost had it all.

All Out of Love

Air Supply

I'm lying alone
with my head
on the phone.
Thinking of you
'til it hurts.

I know you hurt too,
but what else can we do?
Tormented
and torn apart.

I wish I could carry
your smile
in my heart,
for times when my life
seems so low.

It would
make me believe
what tomorrow
could bring,
when today

doesn't really know—
doesn't really know.

I'm all out of love.
I'm so lost without you.
I know you were right
believing for so long.
I'm all out of love.
What am I without you?
I can't be too late
to say that I was so wrong.

I want you to
come back
and carry me home,
away from these
long lonely nights.

I'm reaching for you.
Are you feeling it, too?
Does the feeling seem
oh so right?

And what
would you say

if I called
on you now
and said
that I can't hold on?

There's no easy way,
it gets harder each day.
Please love me
or I'll be gone—
I'll be gone.

I'm all out of love.
I'm so lost without you.
I know you were right
believing for so long.
I'm all out of love.
What am I without you?
I can't be too late
to say that I was so wrong.

Oh, what are you thinking of?
What are you thinking of?
Oh, what are you thinking of?
What are you thinking of?

I'm all out of love.
I'm so lost without you.
I know you were right
believing for so long.
I'm all out of love.
What am I without you?
I can't be too late
I know I was so wrong.

Just Once

Quincy Jones

I did my best,

> but I guess my best wasn't good enough.

> 'Cause here we are, back where we were before.

Seems nothing ever changes.

> We're back to being strangers.

> Wondering if we ought to stay or head on out the door.

Just once,

> can't we figure out what we keep doing wrong?

> Why we never last for very long?

> What are we doing wrong?

Just once,

> can't we find a way to finally make it right!

> To make the magic last for more than just one night?

> If we could just get to it, I know we could break through it.

I gave my all,

> but I think my all may have been too much.

> 'Cause Lord knows we're not getting anywhere.

It seems we're always blowing

> whatever we've got going.

> And it seems at times with all we've got,

> we haven't got a prayer.

Just once,

    can't we figure out what we keep doing wrong?

    Why the good times never last for long?

    Where are we going wrong?

Just once,

    can't we find a way to finally make it right?

    To make the magic last for more than just one night?

    I know we could get through it, if we could just get to it.

Just once.

I want to understand

    why it always comes back to goodbye.

    Why can't we get ourselves in hand and admit to one another:

We're no good without each other?

    Take the best and make it better.

    Find a way to stay together.

Just once,

    can't we find a way to finally make it right?

    Oh, make the magic last for more than just one night?

    I know we could break through it, if we could just get to it.

Just once.

We could get to it.

Just once.

Baby Come Back

Player

Spending all my nights,
all my money, going out on the town.
Doing anything just to get you off of my mind.
When the morning comes,
I'm right back where I started again.
Trying to forget you is just a waste of time.

Baby come back.
Any kind of fool could see
there was something in everything about you.
Baby come back.
You can blame it all on me.
I was wrong, and I just can't live without you.

All day long,
wearing a mask of false bravado.
Trying to keep up the smile that hides a tear.
But as the sun goes down,
I get that empty feeling again.
How I wish to God that you were here.

Baby come back.
Any kind of fool could see

there was something in everything about you.
Baby come back.
You can blame it all on me.
I was wrong, and I just can't live without you.

Now that I put it all together,
give me the chance to make you see.
Have you used up all the love in your heart?
Nothing left for me? Ain't there nothing left for me?

Baby come back.
Any kind of fool could see
there was something in everything about you.
Baby come back.
You can blame it all on me.   53
I was wrong, and I just can't live without you.

I was wrong, and I just can't live.

Our Love Is on the Fault Line

Crystal Gayle

Well, I hear it coming.
    I can feel it in my bones.
And it's weighing heavy on me
    like a sack full of stones.

And I see it in your eyes, baby,
    each time we meet.
And I sense something moving
    underneath our feet.

Baby, our love is on the fault line.
    And you're saying that the fault's mine.
I can't believe that you're so blind.
    Can't believe, can't believe!

You've been stirring up an earthquake.
    You've been cooking up a heartbreak.
And I hope it ain't too late
    for our love. For our love!

Now there's a chilly wind a-blowing
and it's whipping up a gale.
Storm clouds are brewing,
and I know it's gonna hail.

And I see it in your eyes, baby,
each time we meet.
And I sense something moving
underneath our feet.

Baby, our love is on the fault line.
And you're saying that the fault's mine.
I can't believe that you're so blind.
Can't believe, can't believe!

You've been stirring up an earthquake.
You've been cooking up a heartbreak.
And I hope it ain't too late
for our love. For our love!

I feel it in my bones.
I see it in your eyes.
Coming up behind.
Here it comes!
Hold on tight now!

You've been stirring up an earthquake.

    You've been cooking up a heartbreak.

And I hope it ain't too late

    for our love. For our love!

Our love is on the fault line.

    And you're saying that the fault's mine.

I can't believe that you're so blind.

    Can't believe, can't believe!

You've been stirring up an earthquake.

    You've been cooking up a heartbreak.

And I hope it ain't too late

    for our love. For our love!

Our love is on the fault line.

    And you're saying that the fault's mine.

I can't believe that you're so blind.

    Can't believe, can't believe!

How Can You Mend a Broken Heart?

The Bee Gees

I can think of younger days when living for my life
was everything a man could want to do.

I could never see tomorrow, but I was never told
about the sorrow.

And how can you mend a broken heart?
How can you stop the rain from falling down?
How can you stop the sun from shining?
What makes the world go round?
How can you mend this broken man?
How can a loser ever win?

Please help me mend my broken heart, and let me live again.

I can still feel the breeze that rustles through the trees.
And misty memories of days gone by.

We could never see tomorrow. No one said a word
about the sorrow.

And how can you mend a broken heart?

        How can you stop the rain from falling down?

        How can you stop the sun from shining?

What makes the world go round?

        How can you mend this broken man?

        How can a loser ever win?

Please help me mend my broken heart, and let me live again.

Mandy

Barry Manilow

I remember
> all my life
raining down
> as cold as ice.

Shadows of a man,
> a face through a window,
crying in the night.
> The night goes into morning.

Just another day.
> Happy people pass my way.
Looking in their eyes,
> I see a memory:
I never realized
> how happy
> you made me.

Oh Mandy,
> well, you came
and you gave without taking.
> But I sent you away.

Oh Mandy,
> well, you kissed me
and stopped me from shaking
> and I need you today.

Oh Mandy.

I'm standing
> on the edge of time.
Walked away
> when love was mine.

Caught up in a world
> of uphill climbing.
The tears are in my eyes,
> And nothing is rhyming.

Oh Mandy,
> well, you came
and you gave without taking.
> But I sent you away.

Oh Mandy,
> well, you kissed me
and stopped me from shaking
> and I need you today.

Oh Mandy.

Yesterday's a dream.
       I face the morning
crying on a breeze.
       The pain is calling.

Oh Mandy,
       well, you came
and you gave without taking.
       But I sent you away.

Oh Mandy,
       well, you kissed me
and stopped me from shaking
       and I need you today.

Oh Mandy.

The Flame

Cheap Trick

Another night slowly closes in,
    and I feel so lonely.
Touching heat freezing on my skin,
    I pretend you still hold me.
I'm going crazy, I'm losing sleep.
        I'm in too far, I'm in way too deep
            over you.
I can't believe you're gone.

You were the first, you'll be the last.

Wherever you go, I'll be with you.
Whatever you want, I'll give it to you.
Whenever you need someone
to lay your heart and head upon,
remember: After the fire, after all the rain,
I will be the flame.
I will be the flame.

Watching shadows move across the wall,
    I feel so frightened.
I wanna run to you, I wanna call,
    but I've been hit by lightning.

Just can't stand up for falling apart.

    Can't see through this veil across my heart,

        over you.

You'll always be the one.

You were the first, you'll be the last.

Wherever you go, I'll be with you.

Whatever you want, I'll give it to you.

Whenever you need someone

to lay your heart and head upon,

remember: After the fire, after all the rain,

I will be the flame.

I will be the flame.

I'm going crazy, I'm losing sleep.

    I'm in too far, I'm in way too deep

        over you.

You'll always be the one.

You were the first, you'll be the last.

Wherever you go, I'll be with you.

Whatever you want, I'll give it to you.

Rainy Days and Mondays

The Carpenters

Talking to myself
and feeling old.

Sometimes I'd like to quit.
Nothing ever seems to fit.

Hanging around.
Nothing to do but frown.

Rainy days and Mondays always get me down.

What I've got
they used to call the blues.

Nothing is really wrong.
Feeling like I don't belong.

Walking around.
Some kind of lonely clown.

Rainy days and Mondays always get me down.

Funny, but it seems I always wind up here with you.

Nice to know somebody loves me.
Funny, but it seems that it's the only thing to do.
Run and find the one who loves me.

What I feel has
come and gone before.

No need to talk it out;
we know what it's all about.

Hanging around.
Nothing to do but frown.

Rainy days and Mondays always get me down.

Total Eclipse of the Heart

Bonnie Tyler

Turn around.

    Every now and then I get a little bit lonely
and you're never coming around.

Turn around.

    Every now and then I get a little bit tired
of listening to the sound of my tears.

Turn around.

    Every now and then I get a little bit nervous
that the best of all the years have gone by.

Turn around.

    Every now and then I get a little bit terrified
and then I see the look in your eyes.

Turn around, bright eyes.

    Every now and then I fall apart.

Turn around, bright eyes.

    Every now and then I fall apart.

And I need you now tonight.
>And I need you more than ever.
And if you only hold me tight,
>we'll be holding on forever.
And we'll only be making it right,
>'cause we'll never be wrong.
Together we can take it
>to the end of the line.
Your love is like a shadow
>on me all of the time.

I don't know what to do,
>and I'm always in the dark.
We're living in a powder keg
>and giving off sparks.
I really need you tonight.
>Forever's gonna start tonight.
>Forever's gonna start tonight.

Once upon a time I was falling in love,
>but now I'm only falling apart.
There's nothing I can do—
>a total eclipse of the heart.

Once upon a time there was light in my life,
 but now there's only love in the dark.
Nothing I can say—
 a total eclipse of the heart.

Turn around, bright eyes.
 Every now and then I fall apart.
Turn around, bright eyes.
 Every now and then I fall apart.

And I need you now tonight.
 And I need you more than ever.
And if you only hold me tight,
 we'll be holding on forever.
And we'll only be making it right,
 'cause we'll never be wrong.
Together we can take it
 to the end of the line.
Your love is like a shadow
 on me all of the time.

I don't know what to do
 and I'm always in the dark.

We're living in a powder keg
  and giving off sparks.
I really need you tonight.
    Forever's gonna start tonight.
    Forever's gonna start tonight.

Once upon a time I was falling in love,
  now I'm only falling apart.
Nothing I can say—
  a total eclipse of the heart.

She's Gone

Hall and Oates

Everybody's high on consolation.

    Everybody's trying to tell me what is right for me, yeah.

I need a drink and a quick decision.

    Now it's up to me: What will it be?

She's gone, oh, I, oh, I,

I better learn how to face it.

She's gone, she's gone, oh, I, oh, I,

I'd pay the devil to replace her.

She's gone, and she's gone,

oh I, what went wrong?

Get up in the morning and look in the mirror,

    I'm worn as her toothbrush hanging in the stand, yeah.

My face ain't looking any younger.

    Now I can see love's taken her toll on me.

She's gone, oh, I, oh, I,

I better learn how to face it.

She's gone, she's gone, oh, I, oh, I,

I'd pay the devil to replace her.

She's gone, and she's gone,

oh I, what went wrong?

Think I'll spend eternity in the city.

    Let the carbon and monoxide choke my thoughts away, yeah.

Pretty bodies help dissolve the memories.

    They can never be what she was to me.

She's gone, oh, I, oh, I,

I better learn how to face it.

She's gone, she's gone, oh, I, oh, I,

I'd pay the devil to replace her.

She's gone, and she's gone,

oh I, what went wrong?

Alone

Heart

I hear the ticking
of the clock.

I'm lying here.

The room's pitch-dark.

I wonder where
you are tonight.

No answer

on the telephone.

And the night goes by
so very slow.

Oh, I hope that it

won't end and go.

Alone.

'Til now, I always got
by on my own.

I never really cared until I met you.

And now it tears me to the bone.

How do I get you alone?
How do I get you alone?

You don't know
how long I have wanted

to touch your lips

and hold you tight.

Oh, you don't know
how long I have waited

and I was going
to tell you tonight.

But the secret is still my own.
And my love for you is still unknown.

Alone.

'Til now, I always got
by on my own.

I never really cared until I met you.

And now it tears me to the bone.

How do I get you alone?
How do I get you alone?

Making Love Out of Nothing at All

Air Supply

I know just how to whisper,
    and I know just how to cry.
I know just where to find the answers,
    and I know just how to lie.

I know just how to fake it,
    and I know just how to scheme.
I know just when to face the truth,
    and then I know just when to dream.

And I know just where to touch you,
    and I know just what to prove.
I know when to pull you closer,
    and I know when to let you loose.

And I know the night is fading,
    and I know the time's gonna fly.
And I'm never gonna tell you everything I gotta tell you,
    but I know I gotta give it a try.

And I know the roads to riches,
    and I know the ways to fame.

I know all the rules and then I know how to break them,
and I always know the name of the game.

But I don't know how to leave you,
and I'll never let you fall.
And I don't know how you do it—
making love out of nothing at all.

Making love out of nothing at all.
Making love out of nothing at all.
Making love out of nothing at all.

Every time I see you, all the rays of the sun are
streaming through the waves in your hair.
And every star in the sky
is taking aim at your eyes like a spotlight.

The beating of my heart is a drum
and it's lost, and it's looking for a rhythm like you.
You can take the darkness from the pit of the night
and turn it to a beacon burning endlessly bright.

I've gotta follow it because everything I know,
well, it's nothing 'til I give it to you.

I can make the runner stumble.

    I can make the final block,

and I can make every tackle at the sound of the whistle.

    I can make all the stadiums rock.

I can make tonight forever,

    or I can make it disappear by the dawn.

And I can make you every promise that has ever been made,

    and I can make all your demons be gone.

But I'm never gonna make it without you.

    Do you really want to see me crawl?

And I'm never gonna make it like you do—

    making love out of nothing at all.

Making love out of nothing at all.

Making love out of nothing at all.

Making love out of nothing at all.

All Cried Out

Lisa Lisa and Cult Jam

All alone on a Sunday morning.
Outside I see the rain is falling.
Inside I'm slowly dying.
But the rain will hide my
crying, crying, crying.

And you:
Don't you know my tears will burn the pillow?
Set this place on fire 'cause I'm tired of your lies.
All I needed was a simple "Hello."
But the traffic was so noisy that you could not hear my cry.

I gave you my love in vain.
My body never knew such pleasure.
My heart never knew such pain.

And you:
You leave me so confused.
Now I'm all cried out over you.

Over you. All over you.
Never wanted to see things your way.
I had to go astray.

Oh, why was I such a fool?

Why, oh why?

> *Now I see that the grass is greener.*
> *Is it too late for me to find my way home?*
> *How could I be so wrong?*

Leaving me all alone.

Don't you know the hurt will cause an inferno?
Romance up in flames—why should I take the blame?

You were the one who left me neglected.

> *I'm so sorry.*

Apology not accepted.
Add me to the broken hearts you've collected.

Oh, I gave you all of me.
How was I to know
you would weaken so easily?
I don't know what to do.

Now I'm all cried out
over you.

How Am I Supposed to Live Without You?

Michael Bolton

I could hardly believe it
    when I heard the news today.
I had to come
    and get it straight from you.

They said you were leaving.
    Someone's swept your heart away.
From the look upon your face,
    I see it's true.

So tell me all about it.
    Tell me about the plans you're making.
Then tell me one thing more before I go:

Tell me how am I supposed to live without you
    now that I've been loving you so long?
How am I supposed to live without you?
    How am I supposed to carry on
    when all that I've been living for is gone?

I'm too proud for crying.

    Didn't come here to break down.

It's just a dream of mine is coming to an end.

And how can I blame you?

    When I built my world around

the hope that one day

    we'd be so much more than friends.

And I don't wanna know

    the price I'm gonna pay for dreaming.

Even now it's more than I can take.

Tell me how am I supposed to live without you

    now that I've been loving you so long?

How am I supposed to live without you?

    How am I supposed to carry on

    when all that I've been living for is gone?

Didn't We Almost Have It All?
Whitney Houston

Remember when we held on in the rain—
the nights we almost lost it.
Once again,
    we can take the night into tomorrow.
    Living on feelings.
Touching you, I feel it all again.

Didn't we almost have it all
    when love was all we had worth giving?
The ride with you was worth the fall, my friend.
    Loving you makes life worth living.

Didn't we almost have it all
    the nights we held on 'til the morning?
You know you'll never love that way again.
    Didn't we almost have it all?

The way you used to touch me felt so fine.
We kept our hearts together down the line.
A moment
    in the soul can last forever.
    Comfort and keep us.
Help me bring the feeling back again.

Didn't we almost have it all
    when love was all we had worth giving?
The ride with you was worth the fall, my friend.
    Loving you makes life worth living.

Didn't we almost have it all
    the nights we held on 'til the morning?
You know you'll never love that way again.
    Didn't we almost have it all?

Didn't we have the best of times
    when love was young and new?
Couldn't we reach inside and find
    that world of me and you?
We'll never lose it again
    'Cause once you know what love is
You never let it end.

Didn't we almost have it all
    when love was all we had worth giving?
The ride with you was worth the fall, my friend.
    Loving you makes life worth living.

Didn't we almost have it all
    the nights we held on 'til the morning?
You know you'll never love that way again.
    Didn't we almost have it all?

Goodbye to Love

The Carpenters

I'll say goodbye to love.

No one ever cared
if I should live or die.

Time and time again
the chance for love has passed me by.

And all I know of love is how to live without it.
I just can't seem to find it.

So I've made my mind up.
I must live my life alone.

And though it's not the easy way,
I guess I've always known
I'd say goodbye to love.

There are no tomorrows
for this heart of mine.

Surely time will lose
these bitter memories.

And I'll find that there is
someone to believe in
and to live for,
something I could live for.

All the years of useless searching
have finally reached an end.

Loneliness and empty days
will be my only friend.

From this day love is forgotten.
I'll go on as best I can.

What lies in the future
is a mystery to us all.

No one can predict
the wheel of fortune as it falls.

There may come a time
when I will see that I've been wrong.

But for now this is my song.
And it's goodbye to love.
I'll say goodbye to love.

Goodbye to You

Scandal

Those times I waited for you seem so long ago.
I wanted you far too much to ever let you go.
You know you never got by—I feel it, too.
And I guess I never could stand to lose.

It's such a pity to say:
Goodbye to you. Goodbye to you.

Could I have loved someone like the one I see in you?
I remember the good times baby now,
and the bad times, too.
These last few weeks of holding on—
the days are dull, the nights are long.

Guess it's better to say:
Goodbye to you. Goodbye to you. Goodbye to you.
Goodbye to you.

'Cause baby it's over now.
No need to talk about it.
It's not the same.
My love for you is just not the same.

And my heart, and my heart, and my heart can't stand the strain.
And my love, and my love, and my love won't stand the pain.
And my heart, and my heart, and my heart can't stand the strain.
And my love, and my love, and my love.

Goodbye to you. Goodbye to you. Goodbye to you.
Goodbye to you.

Now, could I have loved someone like the one I see in you?
Yeah, I remember the good times baby now,
and the bad times, too.
These last few weeks of holding on—
the days are dull, the nights are long.
Guess it's better to say:
Goodbye to you. Goodbye to you. Goodbye to you.
Goodbye to you.

Goodbye, baby.

So long, darling.

Goodbye to you!

Index of First Lines

About the Poets

All Cried Out

Words and Music by Brian George,
Curtis Bedeau, Gerard Charles, Lucien
George, Paul George, and Hugh
Clarke
Copyright © 1985 by BMG Songs, Inc.,
Mokojumbi Music and Zomba Songs,
Inc.
All Rights for Mokojumbi Music
Administered by Zomba Songs, Inc.
International Copyright Secured
All Rights Reserved

All Out of Love

Words and Music by Graham Russell
and Clive Davis
Copyright © 1980 by Nottsongs
All Rights Administered by Careers-
BMG Music Publishing, Inc.
International Copyright Secured
All Rights Reserved

Alone

Words and Music by Billy Steinberg
and Tom Kelly
Copyright © 1983 Sony/ATV Tunes
LLC
All Rights Administered by Sony/ATV
Music Publishing, 8 Music Square West,
Nashville, TN 37203
International Copyright Secured
All Rights Reserved

Baby Come Back

Words and Music by John C. Crowley
and Peter Beckett
Copyright © 1977 by Careers-BMG
Music Publishing, Inc., Crowbeck
Music, Unichappell Music Inc. and
Mighty Nice Music (BMI)
All Rights for Mighty Nice Music
Administered by Bluewater Music
Corp.
International Copyright Secured
All Rights Reserved

Circles

Words and Music by David Lewis and
Wayne Lewis
Copyright © 1982 ALMO MUSIC
CORP. and JODAWAY MUSIC
All Rights Controlled and
Administered by ALMO MUSIC
CORP.
All Rights Reserved
Used by Permission

Cold Hearted

Words and Music by Elliot Wolff
© 1988 EMI VIRGIN MUSIC, INC. and
ELLIOT WOLFF MUSIC
All Rights Controlled and
Administered by EMI VIRGIN MUSIC,
INC.
All Rights Reserved
International Copyright Secured
Used by Permission

Cuts Like a Knife

Words and Music by Bryan Adams and Jim Vallance
Copyright © 1983 IRVING MUSIC, INC., ADAMS COMMUNICATIONS, INC., ALMO MUSIC CORP. and TESTATYME MUSIC
All Rights for ADAMS COMMUNICATIONS, INC. Controlled and Administered by IRVING MUSIC, INC.
All Rights for TESTATYME MUSIC Controlled and Administered by ALMO MUSIC CORP.
All Rights Reserved
Used by Permission

Didn't We Almost Have It All?

Words and Music by Will Jennings and Michael Masser
Copyright © 1987 BLUE SKY RIDER SONGS and PRINCE STREET MUSIC
All Rights for BLUE SKY RIDER SONGS Controlled and Administered by IRVING MUSIC, INC.
All Rights Reserved
Used by Permission

Don't Cry Out Loud

Words and Music by Carole Bayer Sager and Peter Allen
Copyright © 1976, 1978 by Unichappell Music Inc., Begonia Melodies, Inc., Irving Music, Inc. and Woolnough Music, Inc.
All Rights for Begonia Melodies, Inc. Administered by Unichappell Music Inc.
All Rights for Woolnough Music, Inc. Administered by Irving Music, Inc.

International Copyright Secured   All Rights Reserved

Don't Do Me Like That

Words and Music by Tom Petty
Copyright © 1977 ALMO MUSIC CORP.
All Rights Reserved
Used by Permission

The Flame

Words and Music by Bob Mitchell and Nick Graham
© 1987, 1988 HIT & RUN MUSIC (PUBLISHING) LTD. and RED BUS MUSIC (INTERNATIONAL) LTD.
All Rights for HIT & RUN MUSIC (PUBLISHING) LTD. in the United States and Canada Controlled and Administered by EMI BLACKWOOD MUSIC INC.
All Rights for RED BUS MUSIC (INTERNATIONAL) LTD. Controlled and Administered by WB MUSIC CORP.
All Rights Reserved
International Copyright Secured
Used by Permission

93

Goodbye to Love

Words and Music by Richard Carpenter and John Bettis
Copyright © 1972 HAMMER AND NAILS MUSIC and ALMO MUSIC CORP.
Copyright Renewed
All Rights Administered by ALMO MUSIC CORP.
All Rights Reserved
Used by Permission

Just Once

Words by Cynthia Weil
Music by Barry Mann
Copyright © 1981 Sony/ATV Songs LLC
and Mann & Weil Songs, Inc.
All Rights Administered by Sony/ATV
Music Publishing, 8 Music Square West,
Nashville, TN 37203
International Copyright Secured
All Rights Reserved

Love Is a Battlefield

Words and Music by Mike Chapman and
Holly Knight
Copyright © 1983 by BMG Songs, Inc. and
Mike Chapman Enterprises, Inc.
International Copyright Secured
All Rights Reserved

Love Stinks

Words and Music by Seth Justman and
Peter Wolf
© 1980 CENTER CITY MUSIC
(ASCAP)/Administered by BUG MUSIC
and PAL PARK MUSIC
All Rights Reserved
Used by Permission

Making Love Out of Nothing at All

Words and Music by Jim Steinman
Copyright © 1983 by Lost Boys Music
All Rights for the U.S. and Canada
Administered by Edward B. Marks Music
Company

International Copyright Secured
All Right Reserved
Used by Permission

Mandy

Words and Music by Scott English and
Richard Kerr
Copyright © 1971 by Graphle Music Ltd.
and Screen Gems-EMI Music Inc.
Copyright Renewed
All Rights for Graphle Music Ltd.
Administered in the U.S. and Canada by
Morris Music, Inc.
International Copyright Secured
All Rights Reserved

Maneater

Words by Sara Allen, Daryl Hall and John
Oates
Music by Daryl Hall and John Oates
Copyright © 1982 by Unichappell Music
Inc., Hot Cha Music Co. and Geomantic
Music
All Rights for Hot Cha Music Co.
Administered by Unichappell Music Inc.
All Rights for Geomantic Music
Controlled and Administered by Irving
Music, Inc.
International Copyright Secured
All Rights Reserved

Missing You

Words and Music by John Waite, Charles
Sanford, and Mark Leonard
Copyright © 1984 by Paperwaite Music,
Fallwater Music and Markmeem Music